BEST BIBLE STORIES

Lost in Jerusalem!

LOST IN JERUSALEM!

Jennifer Rees Larcombe
Illustrated by Steve Björkman

CROSSWAY BOOKS • WHEATON, ILLINOIS
A DIVISION OF GOOD NEWS PUBLISHERS

Lost in Jerusalem!
Text copyright © 1992, 1999 by Jennifer Rees Larcombe
Illustrations copyright © 1999 by Steve Björkman
U. S. edition published 2000 by Crossway Books
a division of Good News Publishers
1300 Crescent Street
Wheaton, Illinois 60187

First British edition published 1992
by Marshall Pickering as part of *Children's Bible Story Book.*
This book published as a separate edition entitled *Lost!* in 1999
by Marshall Pickering, an Imprint of HarperCollins Religious,
part of HarperCollins Publishers,
77-85 Fulham Palace Road, London W6 8JB.

Cover design: Cindy Kiple
First U. S. printing 2000
Printed in Hong Kong

ISBN 1-58134-150-4

15 14 13 12 11 10 09 08 07 06 05 04 03 02 01 00
15 14 13 12 11 10 9 8 7 6 5 4 3 2 1

LOST IN JERUSALEM!

Luke 2:41-52

It is a day that Mary and Joseph will never forget—

that awful day when they lost Jesus.
It happened while they were in Jerusalem for the
Passover festival. Everyone in Nazareth had locked
up their shops and houses, and the
whole village had set off together for
the great
feast.

Once a year the Jews would travel from all over
Israel to worship God and celebrate the time
that He had freed them from slavery.

Mary and Joseph walked along with their family
and friends to Jerusalem. In the distance, leading
the long procession, they could see Jesus and all
the other children of the village around Him.

"Look at Him," smiled Mary, "he's only **twelve** and yet **everyone** is **drawn** to Him."

"Always in the middle of a crowd," laughed Joseph. "He's so full of fun, he makes everyone happy."

The festival **flashed** by very quickly. Suddenly it was the last day and everyone was packing up to go home again.

Mary and Joseph were far too busy to notice that Jesus was **missing**. He had gone to say goodbye to people at the temple, and this time He had **gone alone.**

"I feel I really **belong** here, in **My Father's house,**" sighed Jesus as He walked around the beautiful building.

"I wish I could stay here **longer,** learning more about My Father."

It was just then that He heard the angry voices.
A **great argument** was going on in one of the
temple courtyards. Some of the teachers of Israel
were quarreling with each other about God.

They were too busy to notice the young boy walking towards them. He actually knew far more about God than they did.

"Who said that?" demanded the most important teacher of all as he spun around and saw Jesus for the first time. He had asked them a question that was so very, very hard none of them could answer it.

"Come here, boy," snapped the old man. "If you're so clever, you tell us the answer."

All day long the teachers fired questions at Jesus, but He answered them all. "Whoever can He be?" they asked as their white beards wagged in amazement. "He's not like any other boy in the world."

By this time Mary and Joseph had set off for home. They thought Jesus must be walking with His friends or His aunts and uncles. It wasn't until they camped for the night that they realized He was lost.

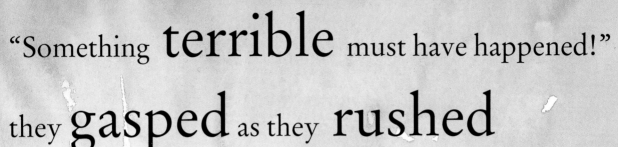

"Something **terrible** must have happened!" they **gasped** as they **rushed** **back** to Jerusalem.

Of course they should have looked for the

Son of God in the temple, but they were so worried they didn't think about that right away. Instead they dashed through the dark streets and noisy markets, searching

desperately.

When at last they *did* look in the temple,

they saw a **strange sight.**

A **vast crowd** had gathered around the old teachers, and in the very center stood Jesus. Everyone was listening to Him in amazement. "Son, why did you scare us like that?" asked Mary. "We thought you were lost."

"You shouldn't have worried about Me," He said gently to Mary. "I had to come to the house of My **real** Father."

"Let's go home. This has been quite a trip to Jerusalem," said Mary.

So Jesus went back to Nazareth and continued to

love and obey

Mary and Joseph.

As He grew older He became wiser, and everybody in town loved Him and respected Him.

Let's talk about the story

1. Why was everyone gathered in Jerusalem?

2. Where did Mary and Joseph find Jesus?

3. Why did Jesus go there?

4. Why were the teachers amazed at Jesus?

5. Where do you feel closest to God?

6. Have you ever been lost, or lost something that was important to you?
   How did you feel?

Awaken Your Soul

by John Drury

FullyAlive360, Inc.
2823 NE 21st Court
Ft. Lauderdale FL 33305
drury@fullyalive360.com
www.fullyalive360.com

All contents ©John Drury, 2005
Edited by Cynthia Green, Thema
Design and layout Maureen Burdock, Thema

First Edition
ISBN number 0-9776985-0-5
Library of Congress Control Number: 2005911403
Printed in Canada

This book is dedicated to my wife, Debbie,
and my daughters, Lauren and Jennie.

SOUL MINER

Your Soul may be buried under old thoughts, habits, fears, and beliefs. The journey of uncovering your Soul is like excavating in a cave. It can be dark, wet, and cold. It can be scary and difficult to navigate if you don't know the way.

Many of us need a guide to help us through this journey. The Soul Miner will show you the way. Shining light on the path. Giving you the tools necessary to do the work. He will be there to support you as you journey into the dark.

This journey is so much about discovery. The deeper you go in, the more you discover.

So I'd like to introduce you to the Soul Miner. He will be your guide. It is my belief that you cannot do this journey alone. You need a guide—or some type of support in your life—to help you navigate the process to Awaken Your Soul.

Enjoy the journey.

CONTENTS

got soul ?

FOREWORD

Soul is your Power.

Soul is our power. It is what makes us a human being. Nourishment and growth of the Soul is why we exist, and it is the part us that is eternal. It is the essence of who we are, and our relationships in life mirror our relationship with our own Soul. False desires like money, power, and sex blind us to our Soul's desire. Feelings of emptiness, boredom, and meaninglessness all expose the loss of Soul, and we can only restore our vision gradually.

For a long time my Soul was asleep. I ignored it. I started my own advertising business in 1980 when I was 26. Over the next 18 years I built the business into a $100 million agency, employing over 100 people. I focused completely on my company. It became my life. I was hooked. I pursued materialistic goals and excluded Soul from my choices. I felt pushed and pulled by what others thought I should be doing, what others thought success meant. I deprived myself of joy, creativity, and true love. Most of the time I operated on "automatic pilot" and I was inattentive to my deeper self, more asleep than awake.

In 1995 I joined YPO (Young Presidents Organization). Eight of us got together and we formed a "Forum Group" to examine our personal and business issues. We decided to have an offsite retreat to get to know one another, and we spent two full days diving inward. This was the first time in my life I had done any internal work and it changed my life.

Through several retreats, I realized that:
- I was a liar.
- I was selfish.
- I was afraid of intimacy.
- I spent my life focused on money, sex, power, and success.
- I did not pay attention to the most important people in my life.

And a whole lot more . . .

I wanted to change and become fully alive. I realized I first had to be honest to my wife, the person I loved most. I had betrayed her many times. When I told her the truth about these betrayals, she left me. This crisis was the catalyst to Awaken My Soul. In order to deal with my crisis, I lived alone and examined the "story" I had created of my life. I realized I was hurrying through life with only ambition and desire. It was empty of Soul and I was miserable. I yearned for healing and meaning. Over the next 4 years I worked hard on making changes in my life—by changing me.

I began to make art and have included much of my work in this book. Many of the pieces explore the painful, dark, difficult parts of life that most of us want to avoid. I think it's important to look at these issues. They are real. They are a part of our lives. Most of us want to pretend they are not there, but they are.

I began to share my story and realized that it isn't just my story; it is the story of so many. When I share what I've experienced, it helps and heals others as well as myself. Looking at the things in life that are hard are the best opportunities for growth even though we don't want to look at our pain or suffering. I want this book to "stir the pot" for you. I want it to keep you thinking and questioning. I want it to help you to ask questions about the things you want to avoid but need to face. At the end of each chapter I've included a series of questions that will help you begin the process of uncovering who you are. I want it to help you uncover your true identity from a Soul level.

For all of us, the journey of life is to uncover our Soul's intent and to feel fully alive. This is the process I have discovered to Awaken Your Soul:

MASKS hide and deny your Soul or give it away to others. Take them off.

RECLAIM the Soul by going inside and exploring those parts of you that have been denied or hidden.

FEEL and connect to your emotions. They are the tools to open the doors to your Soul.

GROW through change, curiosity, and courage.

Like a Soul Miner, delve deep into the dark for your Soul. When you reclaim and awaken your Soul, this is what you can experience:

FAITH that the divine flows within your Soul.

LOVE is not something you do, but who you are.

PASSION as the expression and manifestation of your Soul in your everyday life.

Through my process of Soul Awakening, of becoming Fully Alive, I unleashed the torrent of creativity you see in this book. The process cleanses my wounds and allows me to love. It represents the beauty of the human experience and exposes the raw authentic self that I no longer need to hide and deny. This work is truly from my Soul to yours.

AWAKEN
10

REFLECTIONS GOT SOUL?

1. How do you define Soul?

2. Why are you exploring your Soul at this time in your life?

3. If your Soul had a voice what would it tell you? What does your Soul want?

4. What behaviors, choices, and habits do you engage in that are in direct opposition to what your Soul wants?

5. If you could tell the "story" of your life, what kind of a story would it be? Adventure? Romance? Tragedy? Comedy?

6. What is your unique gift that you offer to the world?

Wake Up

LAYER NO·1

MASKS

MASKS

Awaken Your True Voice!

Wearing masks is a part of how we all survive in the world around us. Most of us spend our entire lifetime—and a lot of wasted energy—displaying different faces to adapt to different environments. I did it all the time. I was so good at it that I couldn't tell the difference between my masks and the "real" me.

Here was my daily routine: Up at 6:00 am. Put on my vain mask and work out. Got to look good. Finish and get dressed. Suit and tie. Put on my "I'm important" mask. Out by 8:00. Work 12 hours. Go home. Then I don my husband and father mask. (Even though I was still mentally at work). Eat dinner, most of the time by myself. Play with the kids for an hour or so, then go into my home office and work until 11:00 or 12:00.

This is how I operated… for 18 years. And I traveled a lot, too.

At the office I wore many different masks. I loved to be in control and wanted it done my way. I wanted people to admire me and to say I was the best. I liked to be the center of attention. I loved to compete and even rationalized cheating and lying to win. I always had to be right. My dreams were always out in front of me. What I had was never enough. Money, sex, power, and success were my focus.

Some weekends I worked. For others I put my family mask back on. On Sunday night I was usually irritable, thinking about all the work ahead of me for the upcoming week, and I would spend Sunday evening, in my home office, preparing for the upcoming week. Oh, yeah, Friday night I would go out with my wife.

Then there was the sexual hunter mask. I used sex as a way to fill a deep empty void inside me. I betrayed my commitment to my wife and had sex outside my marriage. I rationalized it by saying to myself:

- If no one knows, then no one is getting hurt.
- It feels good, and why shouldn't I be able to do things that feel good?
- I can separate sex and love. With these other woman it is just sex. With Deb it's love.
- Other men do it so it's okay. In fact other men think I'm cool because of what I do.

I thought of this as my own world. I wouldn't let anyone in. But it was just another mask. Keeping secrets. Hiding. Playing games. It took a lot of energy from me to wear this mask.

When I look back at those 18 years of my life, I know I wasn't really there. I was not present with my kids or with my wife. Sure, I was physically there, but my Soul was buried under layer upon layer of masks, pretending to be what I wanted others to see or what I thought they wanted to see.

But something felt terribly wrong. I felt empty under all those masks. I felt deeply out of control, driven by voices inside my head that inspired all the faces on the masks, including the voices of my parents and others who influenced me when I was a child. I felt manipulated by fear and desire.

The masks had to go. Peeling them off hurt as much as pulling tape off a tender wound. Healing is painful but that pain Awakens the Soul within.

MASKS hide and deny your Soul or give it away to others. Take them off.
Allow the gift of your true self to unfold.

I want you to accept me.

I want you to like me.

I want you to think I have it all together.

I want you to think I'm smart.

I want you to give me attention.

I want you to think I'm strong.

I want to be seen.

I want you to love me.

I hide behind my masks.

How I Hide

I won't speak up. I stay quiet.
    I'm vague when I say something.
I intellectualize because I don't want
you to know that I don't really know
what I'm talking about.
    I dodge the issue by changing the subject.

I freeze and don't know what to say and
then I make something up.
       I get busy to avoid dealing with
       the issue directly.

I stay distant. I don't call. I avoid you.

    I try and make myself look good
    by putting my issues on you.

       I rationalize.

they can torment me

leave me feeling

helpless

hopeless

empty.

they tell me how to do things

what to do,

when to do it

and what I should think about this or that

there are enough voices

in my head to start

my own choir

MR. RIGHT
COMPETITOR
CONTROLLER
FATHER
LITTLE BOY
TEACHER
LOVER
PLEASER
PUSHER
MR. HUMILITY
MONEY MAN

CRITIC
MANIPULATOR
LIAR
HUNTER
JUDGE
CHEATER
BULLSHITTER
LAZY MAN
WIMP
PREACHER
MR. SELFISH

I'll DO ANYTHING → ANYTHING
TO GET WHAT I WANT

YOU'RE NOT DOING IT GOOD ENOUGH

YOU DON'T OWE ANYBODY ANYTHING

I AM BETTER THAN YOU

BE RESPONSIBLE

YOU CAN DO IT

YOU DESERVE IT

they keep me going with

feelings
worries
hopes
fears and
unresolved dilemmas

YOU ARE ALWAYS RIGHT

CONTROL

YOU'RE A LIAR

(you) DO IT RIGHT

you NEVER DO IT AT ALL (cost

YOU'RE NOBODY.

WIN AT ALL

WORK HARDER

Think of OTHERS

YOU ARE A CHEATER

YOU'RE THE BEST

I JUST WANNA PLAY

YOU CAN'T DO IT

GIVE UP

You're A FAKE

Figure IT OUT

BE FAIR

THE TRUTH

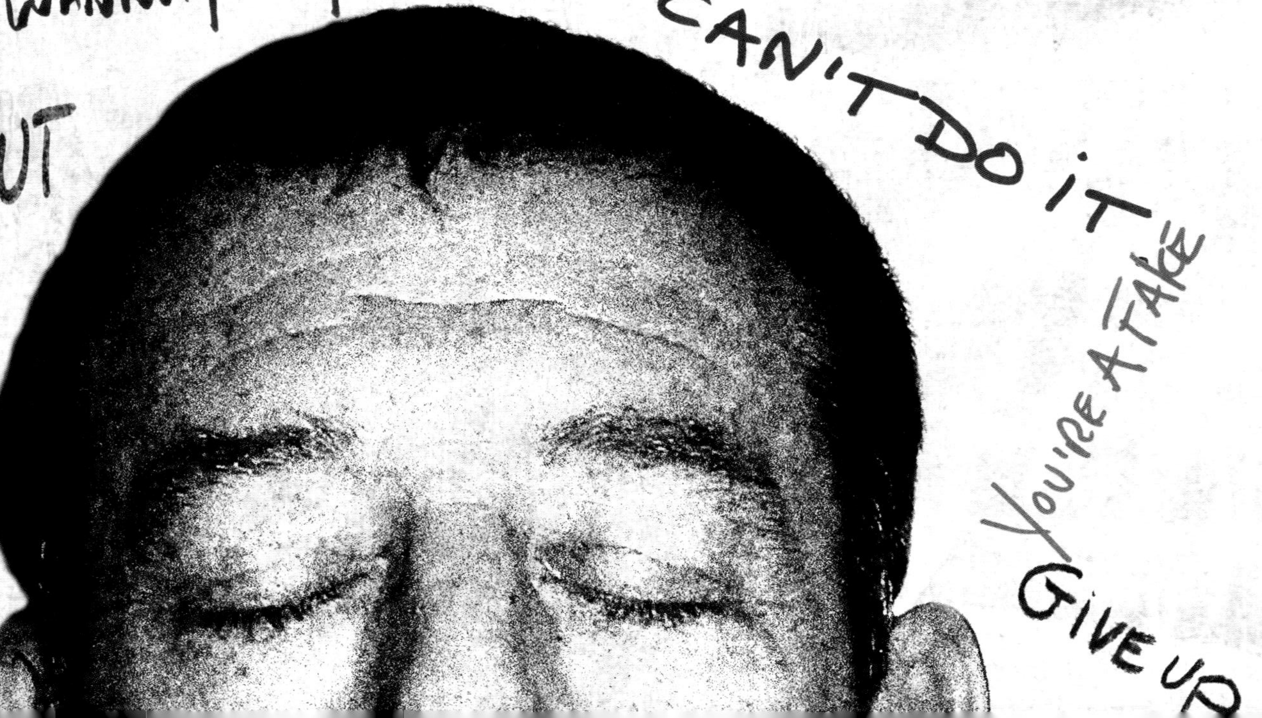

I approached life like a roller-coaster ride. I allowed my life to happen to me. I strapped in, hung on and rode the ups and downs of life.

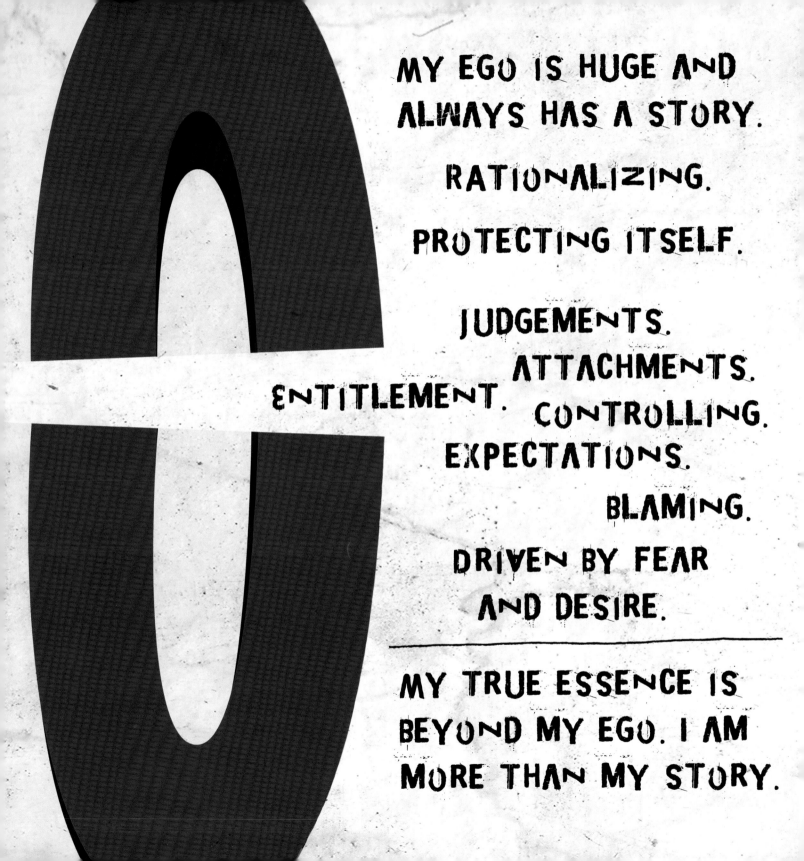

MY EGO IS HUGE AND
ALWAYS HAS A STORY.

RATIONALIZING.

PROTECTING ITSELF.

JUDGEMENTS.
ATTACHMENTS.
ENTITLEMENT. CONTROLLING.
EXPECTATIONS.
BLAMING.

DRIVEN BY FEAR
AND DESIRE.

MY TRUE ESSENCE IS
BEYOND MY EGO. I AM
MORE THAN MY STORY.

My 3 Worlds

there are 3 different places
that i live in. each one serves
me on my journey. i'm beginning
to bring them together to create
one complete picture.

public

this is the part
of me that i show
to the world. the part
that wants to be
accepted and loved
by others. i am
always 'on' in this
world. always wearing
my masks. everything
is always 'GREAT.'

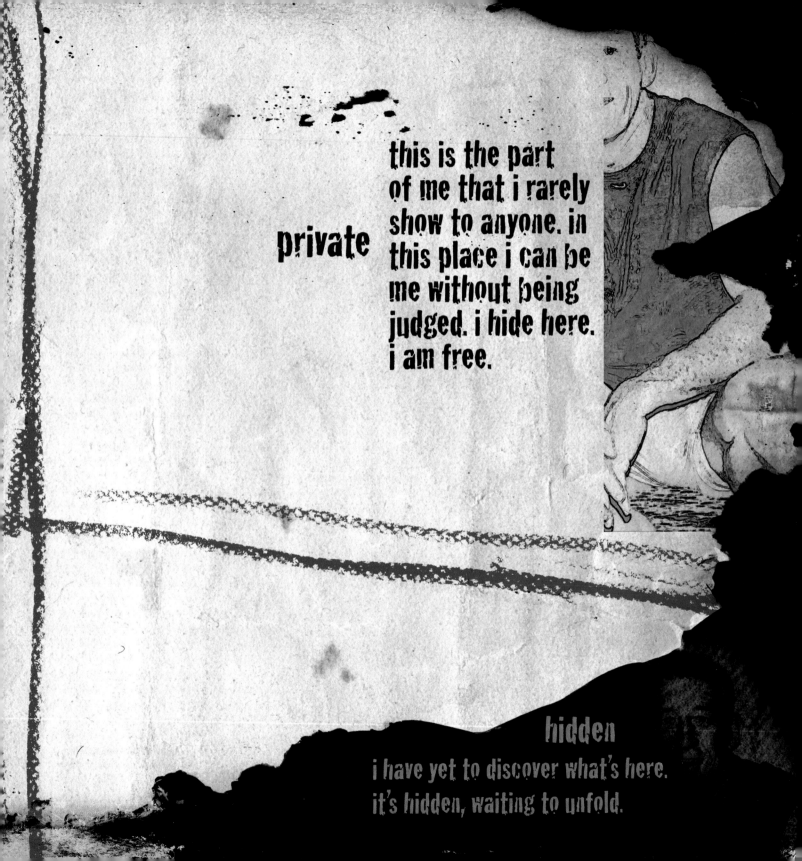

private

this is the part
of me that i rarely
show to anyone. in
this place i can be
me without being
judged. i hide here.
i am free.

hidden
i have yet to discover what's here.
it's hidden, waiting to unfold.

AWAKEN
30

REFLECTIONS
MASKS

1. What labels do you put on yourself? How do you hide behind those labels?

2. What are the two most dominant voices in your head? What do they say to you?

3. What beliefs give you security and run your life? Do you still want them?

4. Do you depend on what others think of you for your self-image and happiness?

5. How do you sacrifice your desires in an attempt to please others?

6. Who are you without labels, masks, or others' opinions of you?

LAYER NO. 2

RECLAIM

RECLAIM

Explore the Hidden Self.

After doing work on the dark side of my nature in retreat, I realized that I had an amazing capacity for joy, love, play, and creativity. The masks had distorted these parts of me and camouflaged my real fear of being rejected and abandoned.

Early in life I covered up those parts of me that were not allowed, loved, or appreciated. As I did my internal work, I discovered that these parts are the essence of who I am and I could get my true power back by reclaiming them. My essence is comprised of all my unopened talents and gifts:

- My vulnerability
- My freedom
- My creativity
- My humility
- My courage
- My compassion
- My sense of wonder
- My spontaneity
- My playfulness
- My love for myself
- My true life's work

These parts required healing. They were crying out for help and they wanted to be released. This healing allowed me to reclaim what I'd denied, buried behind my masks, and disowned.

Keeping secrets is a major roadblock to intimacy and a deep loving connection. The path to intimacy is vulnerability and the path to vulnerability is truth. To find integrity with my wife and myself, I would have to face my biggest fear squarely in the face—the fear of rejection and abandonment—and tell her the truth about my betrayals. So on Oct. 11, 2002, I told her everything about my lies. I was scared shitless. All hell broke lose. She threw me out of the house. My deepest fear was now a reality. I was alone.

My whole life I'd always lived with someone. I had never been alone. I had to push deep down inside to find the self not attached to trying to control the process or run away from it. I cancelled all magazine subscriptions and newspapers; I unhooked the TV. I dedicated myself to mental, physical, emotional, and spiritual work.

I learned to appreciate solitude. It led me to painting, reading, and writing. Day by day, I rediscovered emotions I already had inside of me. I reconnected with the little boy who loves to play and goof around, and the little boy who can cry. I had missed him so much. The masks were so complicated and burdensome. As I shunned them one by one, I reclaimed that simpler, more genuine life. Accessing those parts of myself that I lost has been an exciting part of the journey. I feel fully alive when I allow my true self to show up.

We are all born with an amazing capacity for life. We are joyful, open, loving, authentic, playful, spontaneous, innocent, and full of wonder and beauty. But as we grow up we change. From birth through our early twenties, we spend much of our lives thinking and doing what we learn from our parents, teachers, religions, society, authority figures, and peers. We create masks to protect ourselves, and we learn how to survive in our environment. We stuff, bury, and deny our true self. However, as we get older, those masks no longer work. We have to remove the masks that hide our Souls, go inside, and recover our gifts.

As I worked on my Soul, my wife slowly began to trust me again. After two years, we got back together. We recently celebrated our 30th anniversary.

RECLAIM the Soul by going inside and exploring those parts of you
that have been denied or hidden.

your grandmother says
your dad says:
your mom says:
your grandfather says:
your teacher says:
your brother says:
your sister says:
your priest says:
your friend says:

everyone says

you become?

"I'LL **GIVE** YOU SOMETHING TO CRY ABOUT"

"BIG BOYS DON'T CRY"

"TAKE IT LIKE A MAN"

"DON'T BE A CRYBABY"

"ONLY SISSIES CRY"

No wonder I hold it all in.

freedom

ate

laugh laugh laugh laugh laugh laugh laugh laugh more

The average preschool child laughs over 350 times a day.
The average adult laughs about 10 times a day.
We need to laugh more!!

REFLECTIONS
RECLAIM

1. Do you tell the truth? Where do you avoid telling the truth and why?

2. Is your life balanced? If not, what can you do to regain balance?

3. Are you so busy you feel you are missing a part of your life? Why do you choose to be so busy? What can you do to simplify your life?

4. What part of yourself have you disowned? What wisdom and power does that part offer?

5. When you were in your zone as a kid, what did you love to do most?

6. If you could play right now, what would you do?

FEEL

Emotions move us.

Most men are in their heads most of the time. We haven't been taught how to express our emotions in a healthy way. We hide how we feel from others, even those who are close to us. We are ashamed of emotions like fear, sadness, or shame. All we know is how to deny, rationalize, and ignore our feelings to the point where they become toxic to our mental, emotional, and physical self.

The more we ignore emotions, the louder they get. What we feel emotionally often becomes how we feel physically, and we suffer because we don't know how to seek genuine emotional health. Emotions are an energy that needs to move and can actually harm us if they stay locked up inside. Emotions give us information about ourselves. We can't heal what we refuse to feel.

Our social conditioning distorts our authentic expression of self. We all grew up believing we must be good. We learned that if we disobeyed our parents we would be punished and, worse, deeply disappoint or shame them. There were very limited ways to respond because big boys don't cry and big girls don't get angry. We were taught that expressing our feelings is a sign of weakness.

The voices controlling your emotions and constructing your masks can run your life. They ran mine for a long time. I had to be:

- Mr. Right
- The Competitor
- A Liar
- The Hunter
- The Manipulator
- The Critic

Etc. etc. etc.

In our retreats, I met and embraced these parts of me. They had a gift for me if I was willing to see it. They don't ever go away completely, so I learned how to switch their job from master controllers to advisors. Now I connect to my emotions first, then I listen to the advice of old voices. I decide if I want to take the advice or not. My awakened Soul leads me through my life choices instead of the masks. This realization has helped me in every facet of my life.

I spent most of my life stuffing my emotions and ignoring them. I felt numb, shallow, and empty. I couldn't connect to anyone else because I didn't connect with myself. I didn't give my daughters the right attention for 17 years. I feel sad and guilty about that, but I can begin to change it now.

In the past I was committed to work. I was committed to making money. I was committed to getting sex. I was committed to success. Now it's different. I have allowed myself to express my emotions openly and freely. I'm committed to working out four times a week to take care of my body. I'm committed to eating a healthy diet. I'm committed to spending time with my two daughters. I'm committed to my relationship with my wife. I'm committed to doing my personal work and to trust the process. I'm committed to listening to my feelings. I'm committed to making different choices in my life that nourish and expand my Soul.

Feelings are always flowing through us. They are the expressions of our Soul and are neither positive nor negative. Feelings are the raw material for becoming fully alive. Through the creative outpour that came about when I removed my masks, I reclaimed joy, love, play, and creativity but also sadness, guilt and shame, fear, and anger. I learned:

- Embracing sadness can help you develop compassion
- Guilt and shame give you a sense of conscience
- Facing fear motivates action
- Anger is the raw material for developing boundaries in healthy relationships

There is great wisdom in our emotions. We need to learn to value them and realize the gift we get when we are emotionally alive. **FEEL** and connect to your emotions. They are the tools to open the doors to your Soul.

I find it hard to connect to my heart.

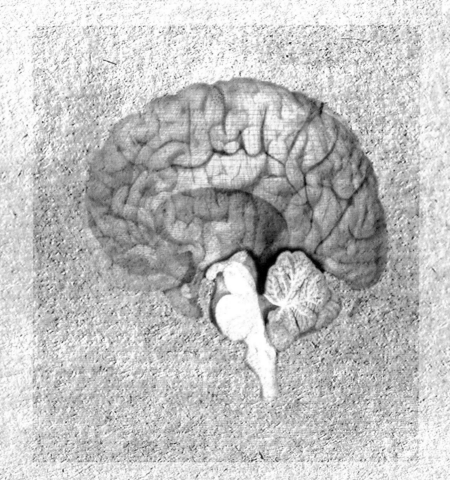

I'm over here most of the time.

Rationalizing. Thinking things through.
FigUring it out.

StEPs to HAPPinEss

1. **finish school** (from a good one)

2. **get a job** (a good one)

3. **get married** (to a good one)

4. **start your own business** (work hard)

5. **have 2.5 kids** (get a dog)

6. **buy a a big house** (and a lot of other stuff)

p y

(mid-life crisis in here somewhere)

7. work harder (to pay for all the stuff)

8. sell out to somebody (big bucks)

9. go back to #3 (to a younger one)

10. consult, dabble alittle

11. retire (now what)

p

is this what it's really about?

sOME
    DAYS I
  JuST FEEL
LiKE
     LEAViNG
  iT ALL

   JuST
  FUCK iT

Anger
is my
FEAR
ANNOUNCED

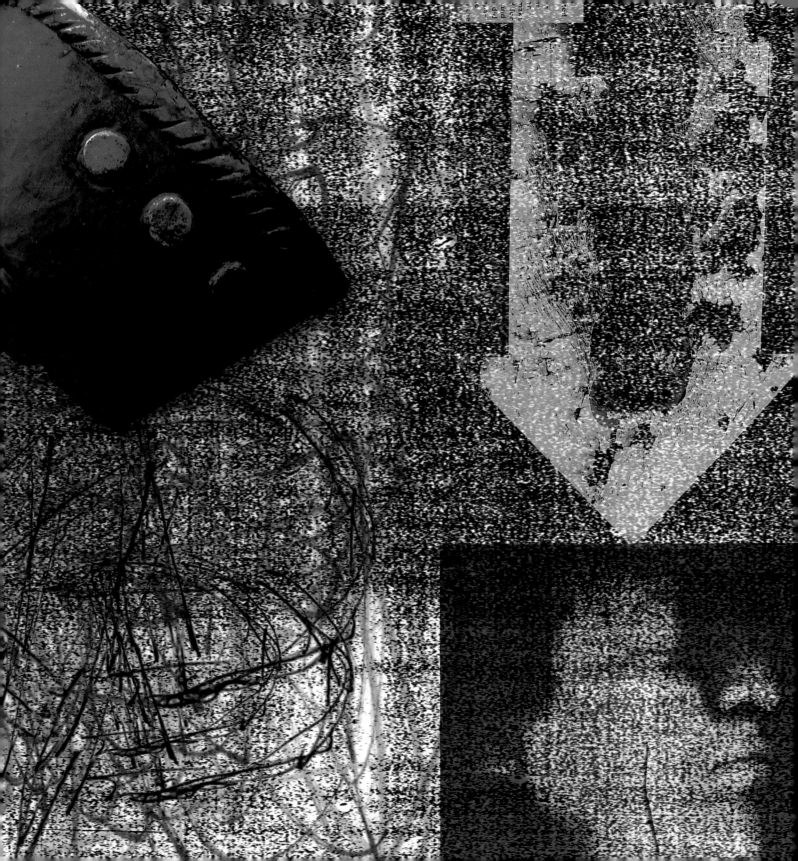

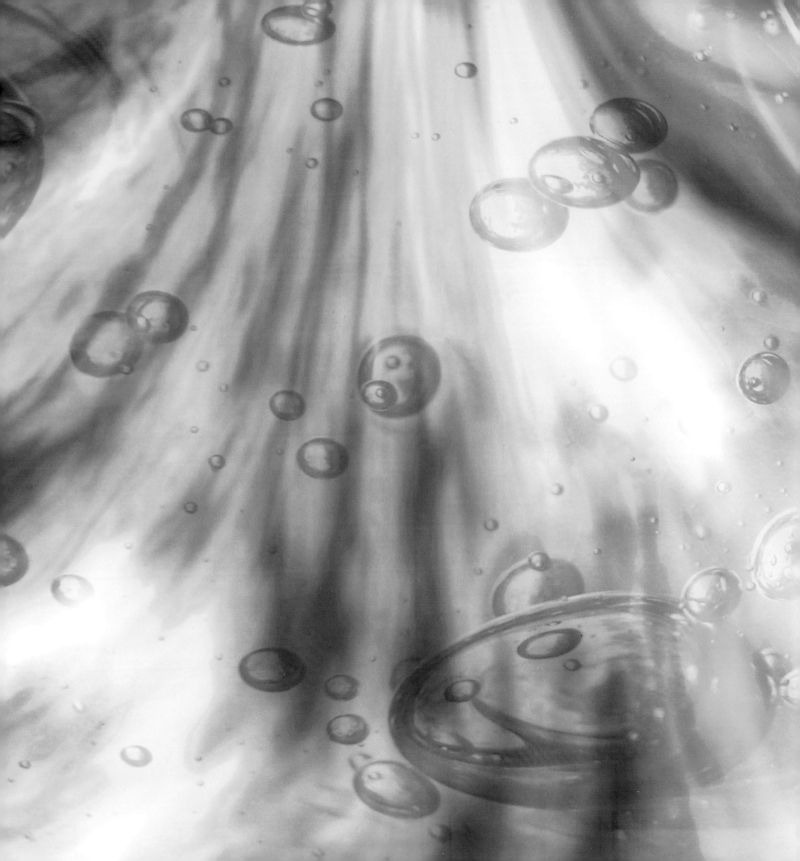

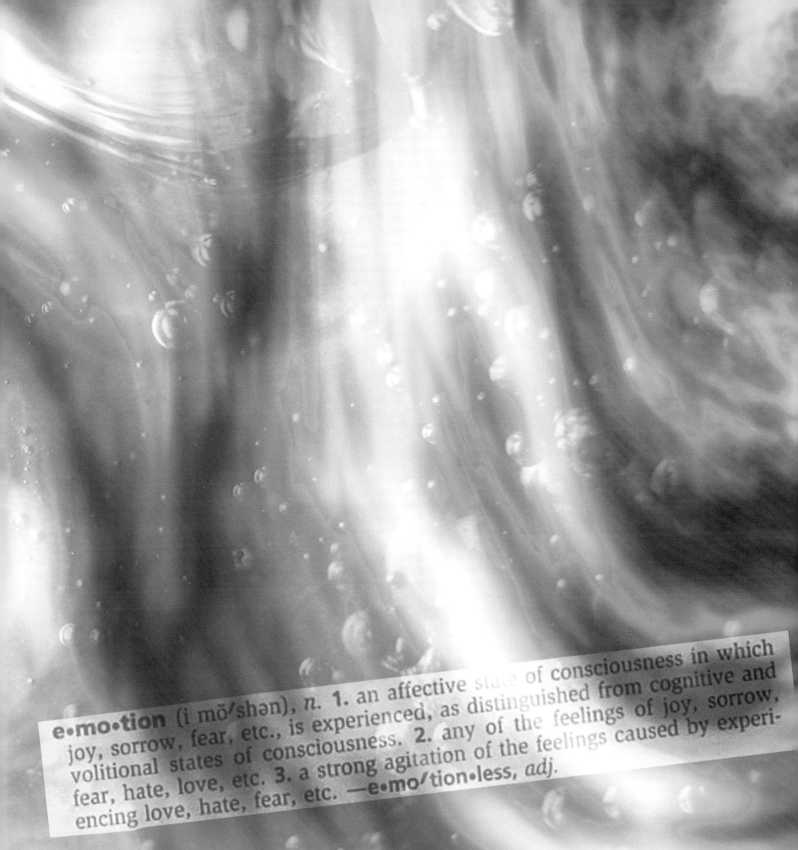

e·mo·tion (i mō/shən), *n.* **1.** an affective state of consciousness in which joy, sorrow, fear, etc., is experienced, as distinguished from cognitive and volitional states of consciousness. **2.** any of the feelings of joy, sorrow, fear, hate, love, etc. **3.** a strong agitation of the feelings caused by experiencing love, hate, fear, etc. —**e·mo/tion·less,** *adj.*

AWAKEN
66

REFLECTIONS
FEEL

1. Do other people understand your emotions?

2. How do you express your feelings in healthy ways? In unhealthy ways?

3. Do you stuff your emotions? If so, why? Where do you hold your stuffed emotions in your body?

4. What are your three greatest fears? Where do they come from? How do they manifest in your life? What is the worst that can happen if your fears come true? What do you do to conquer your fears?

5. Do you sometimes feel angry? What is the fear underneath your anger?

6. What gives you joy?

GROW

Dance With Change.

Life is about growth, movement, and change. It is the way the universe unfolds. We can learn to accept and embrace it, or fight it. We can learn to find the gift embedded in change, or become its victim. We can face change with curiosity and courage, or doubt and fear. We can learn to dance with change, or kick it in the teeth.

I was taught "how to be successful in life." I was told that if I followed that path I would be happy. Every time I accomplished a goal I created a bigger goal. I never had enough. I believed that my financial achievements were the benchmark for measuring success and for measuring the value of who I was as a person. Our culture equates who we are with what we do. I calculated growth only in monetary terms and I was afraid to fail. There was no balance between a life well lived and a life lived for work, and I fell victim to an addictive cycle: accomplish this; be that; work harder.

My personal growth required a whole new process. For most of my life I did not believe I was creative in the sense of being able to express my self in the arts. The deep fear I had was that people would laugh or criticize any form of creative expression. So I buried my creativity under the mask of accomplishment.

When I was alone—when Deb and I were separated—I decided that I'd try painting in spite of my fear. A book by Sark inspired me to try painting with watercolors. I went to an art supply store one afternoon, bought some paints, and I started that night. I choose to paint hearts and crosses partly because they were easy. Painting was a gift to myself. Though the compositions were simple, they expressed something authentic.

I explored different ideas that I got out of books and my emotions. I expressed them through my artwork. I could clearly see the piece in my head, but still had difficulty expressing it exactly the way I wanted it to look. So I bought an Apple computer and hired Angelo, a freelance artist, to teach me how to use Adobe Photoshop. I learned this new tool for creative expression after work and on weekends.

Now the work was coming together the way I envisioned. I scanned in my paintings and created layers of words, color, texture, and meaning. I decided that I didn't care what others thought of my artwork. I felt great curiosity about where the designs would lead. I did this as a form of therapy, a way to Awaken My Soul. Over the course of a year I grew in leaps and bounds until I was able to get out the emotions and visions I felt deep inside. The creative work changed me and helped me unfold the deepest level of myself.

When I was thrown on the road to becoming fully alive, I became curious about the person under my masks. I began to dance with change instead of kicking at life like an angry child. Painting, writing, and reading began to heal my psyche. I pushed through my success mask and used a different blueprint for achievement.

I was able to **GROW** through change, curiosity, and courage.

We create a nest.

Its cozy **safe**
comfortable **predictable**
convenient

We venture out each day to work
and do our chores.

We return to eat, watch TV
and sleep.
Same thing next day.
next day.
next day.
next day.
next day.

What keeps us stuck in
a limited view of reality?

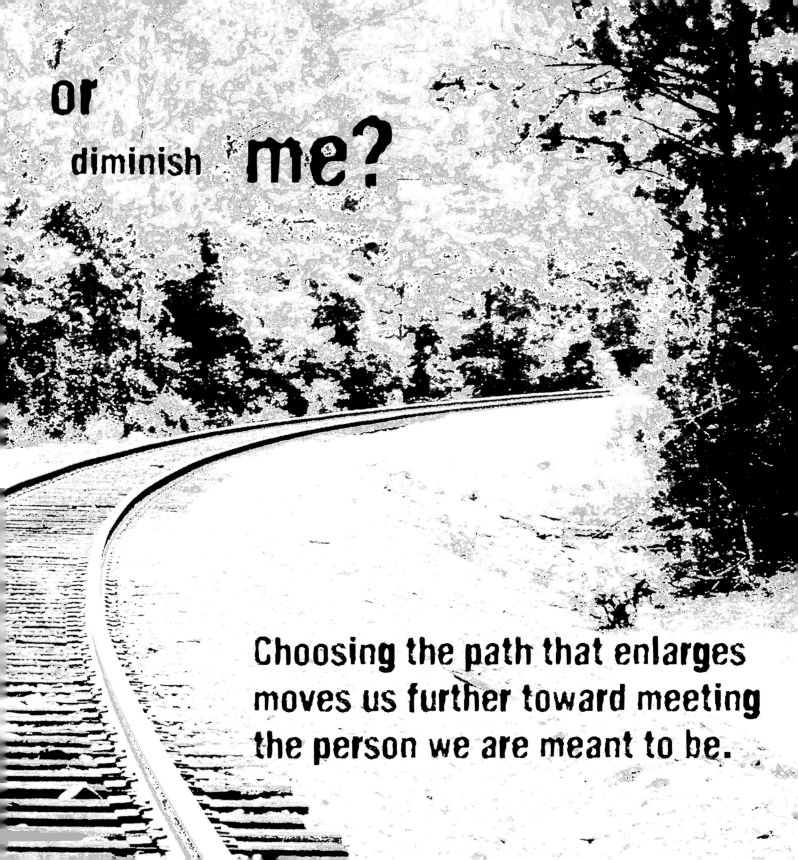

or
diminish me?

Choosing the path that enlarges moves us further toward meeting the person we are meant to be.

I SEE THE WORLD THROUGH
THE LENS OF MY BELIEFS.

SO WHAT I SEE AROUND ME
IS WHAT I HAVE INSIDE ME.

IF I WANT TO ALTER WHAT
I SEE HAPPENING AROUND ME,

I HAVE TO CHANGE THE FILTER.

TOUGH TO DO.

Let go of the past and heal your Soul.

Easy to say. Hard to do.

Even though it's painful, we hold onto the past.

We hold onto emotional wounds that keep us
trapped in the past. The glue that holds us to
these wounds includes; resentment, shame, anger,
fear, sadness, blame, regret, envy, jealousy,
loneliness, and self-pity.

I believe that these wounds have a gift for us.
If we are willing to take the time to honor and
heal these issues from our past we can learn a
great deal of wisdom from the pain we carry.

The key is not to get rid of our past,
but to integrate it into our lives and get
our freedom back.

Or we can just keep on living
in the past and miss out on all
the wonderful things that are
right in front us.

PAIN DEEP

AND REV

TO YO

PAIN LE

POSSI

ENS YOU

EALS YOU

URSELF

ADS TO

BILITY

BE
OPE
TO
CHAN

AWAKEN
84

REFLECTIONS
GROW

1. What baggage do you carry from the past?

2. What unhealthy commitments do you have? How do they hold you back?

3. What behaviors do you want to change? What single behavior do you want to change right now?

4. What is the block you create that prevents the change you want in your life?

5. How do you express your creativity? How can your creativity help you change?

6. What gift do you want to give yourself right now?

LAYER NO. 5

FAITH

FAITH

The Vast Place of Not Knowing.

After removing Masks to Reclaim my Soul, Feeling with depth, and Growing, I rediscovered the meaning of Faith. For most of my life I've misunderstood the journey of faith. When I was a child, I used to go to Mass every day, attend religion classes, and confess. I was an altar boy; I answered to priests and nuns. It was pounded into my head that, if I was always "good" in the eyes of God, I would go to heaven. If I was "bad" I could go to hell. It's been hard to change the fear-based beliefs of my Catholic upbringing. In order to be part of a religion, I had to comply with someone else's dictates about God. I conformed to their vision of spiritual truth and lived most of my life in fear of God.

Because of the fear inherent in the good/bad model of spirituality, I disconnected from a relationship with God. The pain I've experienced in the process of becoming fully alive has awakened a desire to better understand my spirituality. I felt like I was in hell and didn't want to go back.

Through art, writing, and reading, I've taken the time to clean out a lot of old pipes to make room for new thinking. As I've rediscovered my Soul, I've questioned, wondered, and explored. Sometimes I want proof that God is there. I want direct answers to my questions. Why do certain things happen to the people I love? Why is there so much pain in the world? But the answers don't come in plain English. I've had to find a new concept of faith.

I know that something has helped me through my pain, my hell. Something has guided me, supported me, and even loved me. I call it Angels. I believe they are messengers of God and they've helped me restore my faith. They are always there. God is always there. Everywhere.

In solitude, within the new relationship with my wife, by the creation of original art, and through the redefinition of my achievement in work, I've enjoyed everything in life more. My Soul is open and relaxed. I've been able to let some of the symbols of my religion become the symbols of my new spirituality. They are part of me and they are very beautiful! I've allowed myself not to know exactly what they mean and not to fear them. In letting go of answers, I've found the divine again. Faith is about relaxing into the vast place of not knowing.

FAITH is the divine spirit that flows within your Soul.

God...God...
where are you?
sometimes i question?
do you hear me...at all

faith...faith...faith

silence

JUDGEMENTAL
ANGRY!
I WAS TAUGHT TO
FEAR GOD. DEMANDING

JUDGEMENT DAY!
GOD is WAY up here somewhere
In the heavens separate for me.

GOD

GOD is Almighty --- All powerful

LIMBO is where?

Be good
OBEY the commandments
READ the bible PRAY!

WATCH OUT!

VENIAL SINS
↓
PURGATORY is over
HERE SOME WHERE

ME →
BEING PULLED
BY BOTH POWERS
(AND GOD could lose
the BATTLE for my Soul)

FREE Will
I have a FREE Will.
However If I EXERCISE
IT IN A WAY THAT GOD
DOESN'T LIKE .....THEN
I'm SCREWED.

MORTAL SINS
↓
HELL
DAMNATION FOREVER

SATAN OR DEVIL
TEMPTING ME TO DISOBEY THE
Will of GOD

still searching

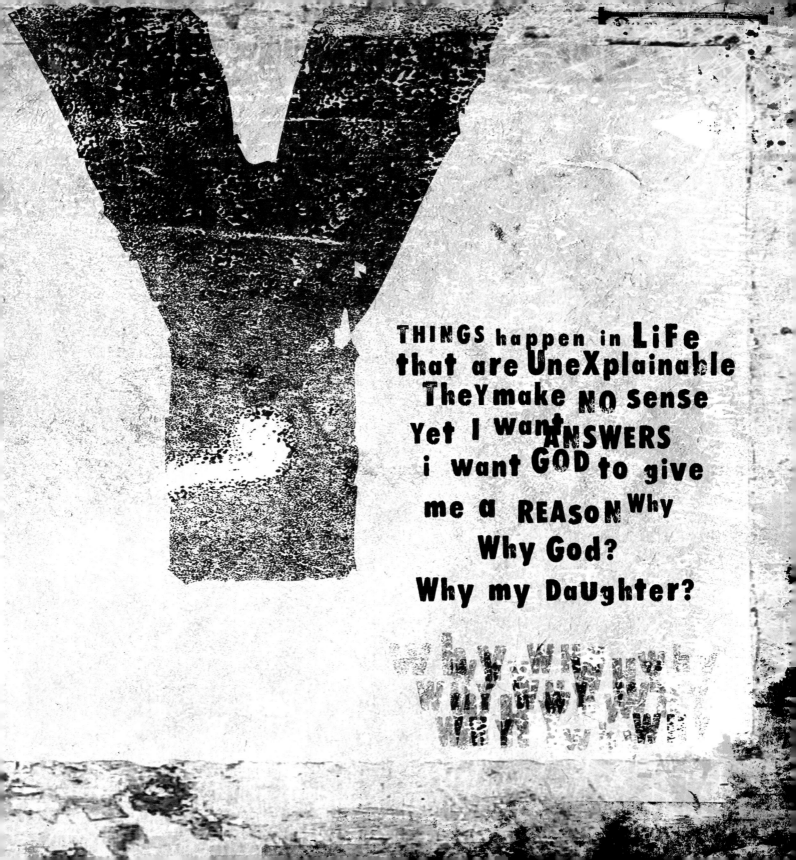

Y

THINGS happen in LiFe
that are UneXplainable
TheY make NO sense
Yet I want ANSWERS
i want GOD to give

me a REASoN Why

Why God?

Why my DaUghter?

i believe in angels

they show up in my life in a
number of different ways

they help me with answers

they help me see

they guide me

they love me

they hold me when i'm in pain

they are always there

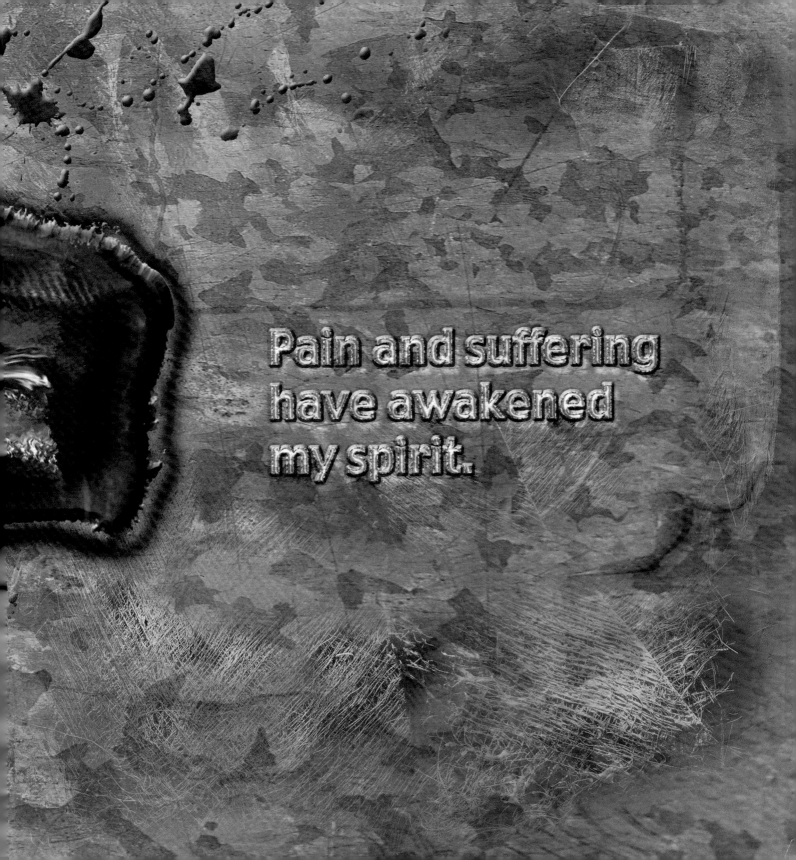

Pain and suffering have awakened my spirit.

God's right here

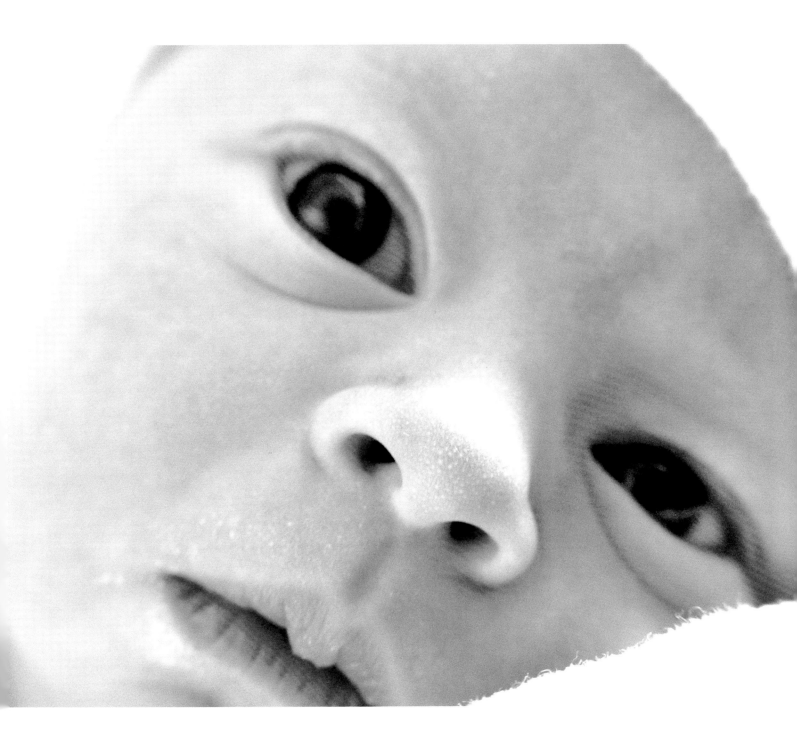

AWAKEN
102

REFLECTIONS FAITH

1. What is the difference between religion and spirituality for you?

2. What role does spirituality play in your life?

3. What form of spiritual practice or discipline do you have in your life?

4. What do you do when you are in emotional pain?

5. What do you do when you are in spiritual pain?

6. How do you connect with your spiritual self? What is your dark side? What is your light side?

LAYER NO. 6

LOVE

LOVE

Life is About Love.

Love can hurt. I have been hurt and I have done my share of hurting. For a long time I thought that love was just about sex and being happy. I erected armor around my heart to protect myself from the pain of rejection. I locked myself in really tight. It was too big a risk for me to take off the armor and to be vulnerable. When relationships went bad, I blamed it on others.

I didn't understand Love. I thought I knew what it was. I connected love to doing things. Giving attention, giving gifts, being a good lover, being a good provider, etc. I had to look inside my heart before I could get clarity about relationships. I'm the only one who knows how and why I locked myself up, and I'm the only one who has the key to unlock my heart.

Love is not something you do; it is who you are. Love is an energy that flows through all of life. This was a new idea for me. I had to learn to love myself before I could truly love others. I had to learn how to experience and practice self-love. Love who I am. Love what I've done. Love my gifts and my faults. Love my body as it is. Love what I do. Love it all. Then I could let this love flow out to others.

To get to this love for myself I had to forgive myself. Look at all the guilt, blame, and resentments I held against myself. I judged myself harshly for being bad, making mistakes, hurting others or what I could have done better. I held onto these self-judgments and carried them for years. Forgiveness is essential if I want to find happiness and joy. I learned to let go. To forgive myself. This process of learning how to forgive myself allowed me to learn how to forgive others in my life as well.

Love is about feelings. I had to learn how to get in touch with my feelings and give myself permission to feel all of my emotions. To connect with my joy, sadness, fear, shame and anger.

I had to let myself be vulnerable and let the pain in. I had to conquer my fear and accept that pain and suffering are an inevitable part of life. All emotions are important and all need to be recognized. Real power comes from being vulnerable enough to feel what's inside.

In reclaiming many buried aspects of my Soul, I've rediscovered the necessary ingredients for deep love:

- Humility
- Patience
- Self-love
- Vulnerability
- Intimacy
- Thinking with my heart
- Accepting pain

As with my newfound concept of faith, I wanted to build a new model for love. Some spiritual practices believe that we are all one. All connected. I like the idea that we're all unique yet connected. We're interdependent, and what we give is inseparable from what we receive.

For years, I wanted my wife, Debbie, to fit into my idea of love. I wanted her to love me the way I wanted to be loved. This was not love; this was my insecurity in full bloom. It was about me getting my needs met. As I did my personal work I realized that Debbie was a mirror for me in our relationship. If I was open and willing, I could see those parts of me that I didn't like unfold between us. This allowed me to learn how to be more conscious of my relationship and myself. It changed how I experience Debbie and how we experience Love in our relationship.

I've learned that Love is about freedom. It is about letting Deb be the person she chooses to be, not the person I want her to be. I accept and support her chosen path, instead of only supporting mine.

One day I took all the cards that my wife had sent me over the years and I made a composite of her love for me. I feel her love all over the pages. I love it. And I love her.

LOVE is not something you do, it is who you are. Love is Life.

i hurt when i feel the arrows of resentment.

i hurt when i avoid the truth.

i hurt when i grieve.

Love can hurt.

i hurt when i don't follow my heart.

i hurt when i'm alone.

i hurt when i'm rejected.

i hurt when i see others in pain.

Some days.

There are days when I feel my heart is wide open.

This feeling comes from within me.
I feel in love.   My life is perfect.
She is my soulmate.   My heart jumps when I see you.
                        My heart dances when I feel this way.
I want this to last forever.   It feels amazing.
                   I always have access to this love.
I feel connected.
                   I feel accepted.

Other days.

There are days everything feels upside down and I close my heart because I'm afraid of getting hurt.

I feel lonely.   I feel rejected.
Life sucks.   I think that love is outside of me.
I feel sad.   It feels like it's never going to work.
    My heart feels heavy.   She doesn't understand me.
                I hurt inside.

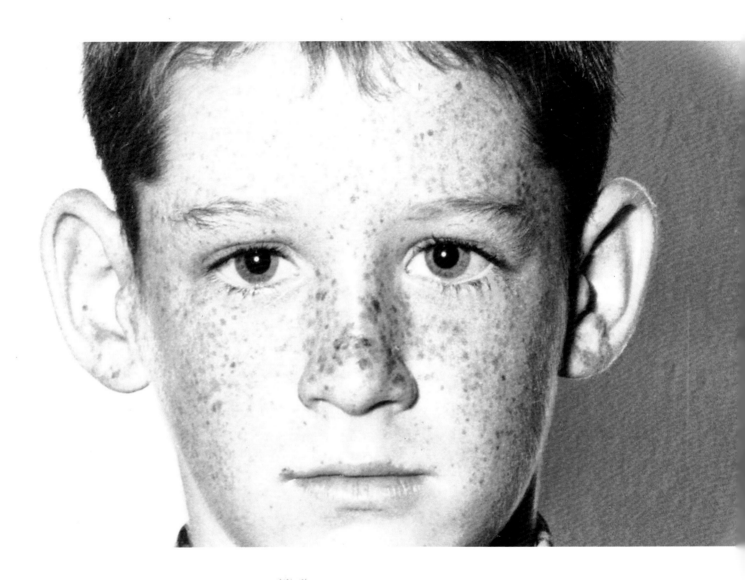

I'M AFRAID OF
THE GIFT YOU
HAVE FOR ME.

I needed ya. Share with me
I got ya. the events of each day,
the pleasures of each night.
I'm keeping you my partner,
my best friend.
Love ya. my love.

I'm strong for you

Love U,
Me

Forever
Me

Dear Israel

Your kindness
is appreciated
more than words can
say.

Thank You.

Walk with me
through the
seasons.
Talk with me
through all
that life may bring
our way. Travel
with me to the places of
our
dreams.

Our special love

is something my heart

will never take

for granted.

I love you   Mean So Much

Happy Birthday   to Me

Thank you for listening.
Thank you for giving.
Thank you for helping me
grow.
All my love me

I love you being with you. You do
spoil me, I am so lucky!

me   I love I love
you

Forever   All my love
me   Debbie

J. D. + D. D.

Love you.

me (Boopy)

I believe in our love, in hopeful dreams, and in all that is yet to be because I believe in you.

All my love & kisses
xoxoxo
me

Happy Anniversary to My Wonderful Husband

Happy Birthday

I love you with all my heart. Thank you

Dearest John,

all my love
everything

I love U With All My ♥!

me

When I am away from you,
I am still with you.
When my eyes are closed,
I still see you.
When I am awake,
I still dream of you.
When I feel I have everything,
I still need you.
And no matter what,
I will always love you.

INSPIRED BY SPANISH POETRY

Congrats !!! Hope you make it!!!

I love you.

what I wouldn't do to lick your earlobes.

Thank you "Teacher"

All my love

me

Boopy

Everyone is unique.
Everyone is connected.

REFLECTIONS
LoVE

1. How do your relationships fall apart?

2. Are you willing to take 100% responsibility for the problems in your relationships? Where do you take less than 100%? Why? Where do you take more? Why?

3. What do you see in others that you like? What pushes your buttons?

4. What fears do have about love? What's the risk of not loving?

5. Who do you have to forgive to move on?

6. What gifts do people close to you offer you?

LAYER NO. 7

PASSION

PASSION

Music of the Awakened Soul.

Oliver Wendell Holmes observed that most of us die with our music still inside us. But we don't have to! I am creating a life the way I want it to be. I have gone inside and opened a path for my personal gifts to come forth into the world. I pay attention to the things that stimulate me, make me playful, make me creative because these things nourish me and make me capable of love. This passion for life is the music of my awakened Soul.

If you are not currently doing what you love to do, going into new territory is frightening. It takes courage and faith to step away from the comfortable and familiar and step into your passion. So much more can be made of life than the whirring repetition of old patterns, old thoughts, and old worries. If thoughts are the gateway to your destiny, then you can't get there clutching safe but limiting beliefs.

Clues to your passion are in your dreams. Revisit the dreams of your childhood. They hold the seeds of your Soul. As you grew up, you buried those dreams under the weight of criticism and negativity and scorn. You protected yourself, donned masks, and lost faith in your own voice. Those dreams are still there. Reject the negative conditioning. Resurrect the dreams for they hold the source of your passion.

Passion is not a privilege of the fortunate few; it is a right and a power that we all possess. You might envy those who are fired up about their lives. You might view their success as the product of luck or circumstance, but rarely does either play a factor. Those who reap the rewards of following their passion do so because they make a conscious choice to integrate it into their lives. When you act in opposition to your heart, defying your passion, you are left with feelings of emptiness and longing. When you rule out passion, you introduce yourself to a life of regret, a life of what-ifs.

Deciding to follow your heart entails risk. Only you can decide how you will let your passion guide you. Why is this so important? Because passion is the core of you—it is who you are. Passion is the manifestation of that unique potential that we all have inside us. It is the key. Passion gives you life.

It took me over twenty years before I recognized the relationship between my head and heart. I was taught to defer to my head in all matters. I could analyze, figure out, rationalize, manipulate, and justify anything. I was in my head all the time and rarely in my heart. I now know that the key is to start with my heart then use my head to give shape and substance to my dreams.

I learned the most important lesson of life: you find true joy and happiness by connecting with what's inside, not outside. I thought that money, success, prestige, power, status, nice house, blah blah blah would make me happy. They don't. I'm happy when I'm doing what I love to do. Which for me is this. Teaching and sharing with others. This is my passion. And for me Passion Rules!

Tap into that passion and you will love life. **PASSION** is the expression and manifestation of your awakened Soul in your everyday life.

It's our comfort zone. We just keep going around in circles. We want things to be safe, secure and predictable.

While our dreams are over here.

(Break out and fly)

Courage to be me.

Courage to tell the truth.

Courage to be vulnerable.

Courage to surrender to God.

Courage to follow my passion.

Courage to go through my deepest fears.

When we come to the edge

Of all the light we have

And we must take a step into

The darkness of the unknown,

We must believe one of two things:

Either we will find something firm to stand on

Or we will be taught to fly.

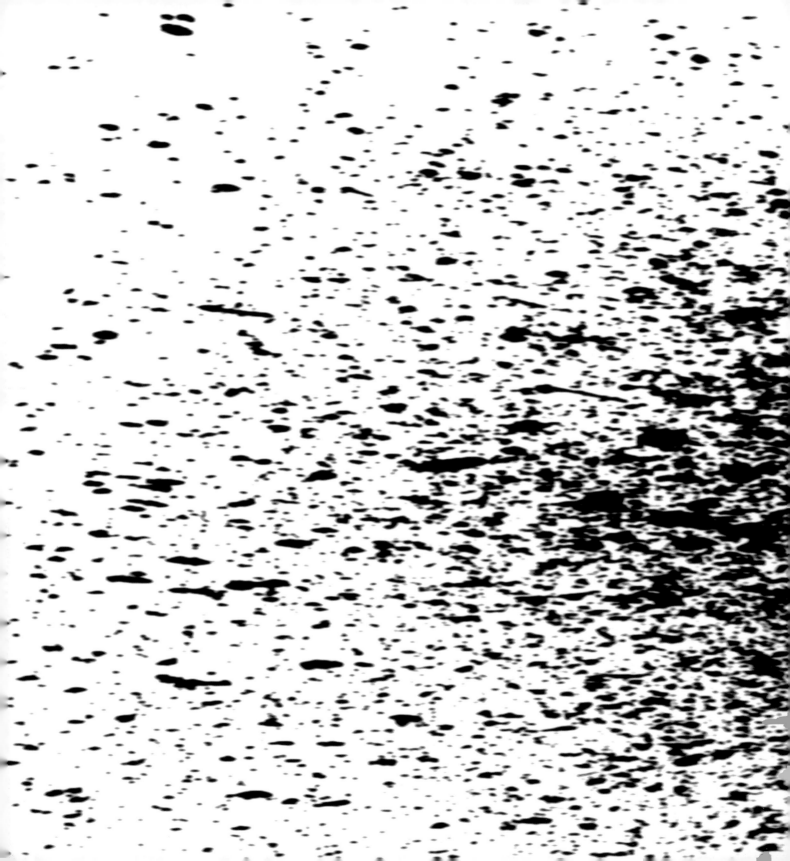

STEP OUT INTO THAT BIG SPACE.

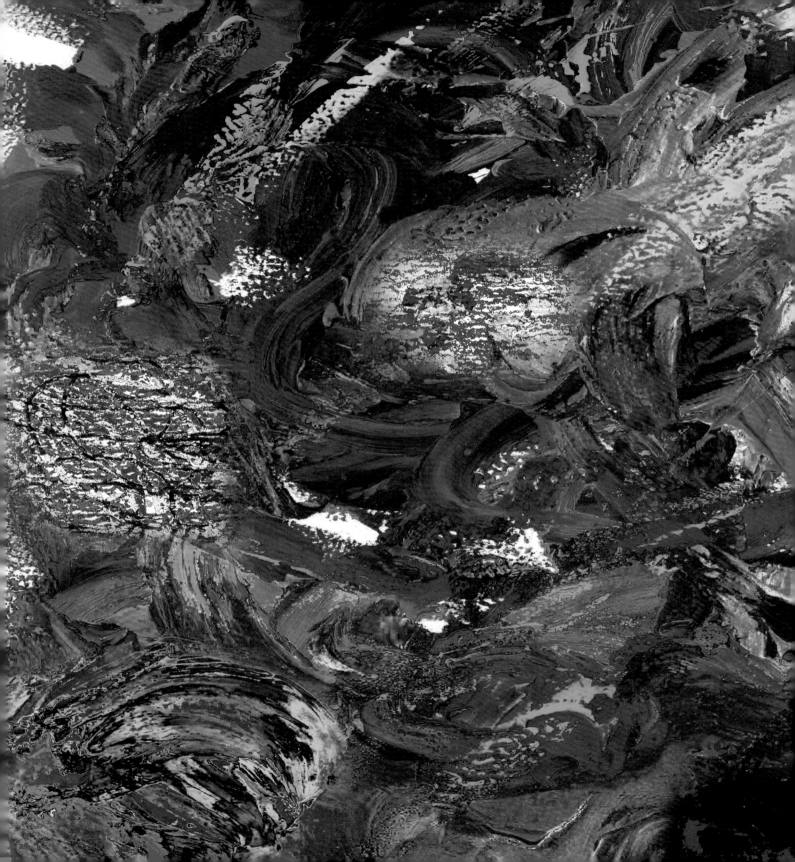

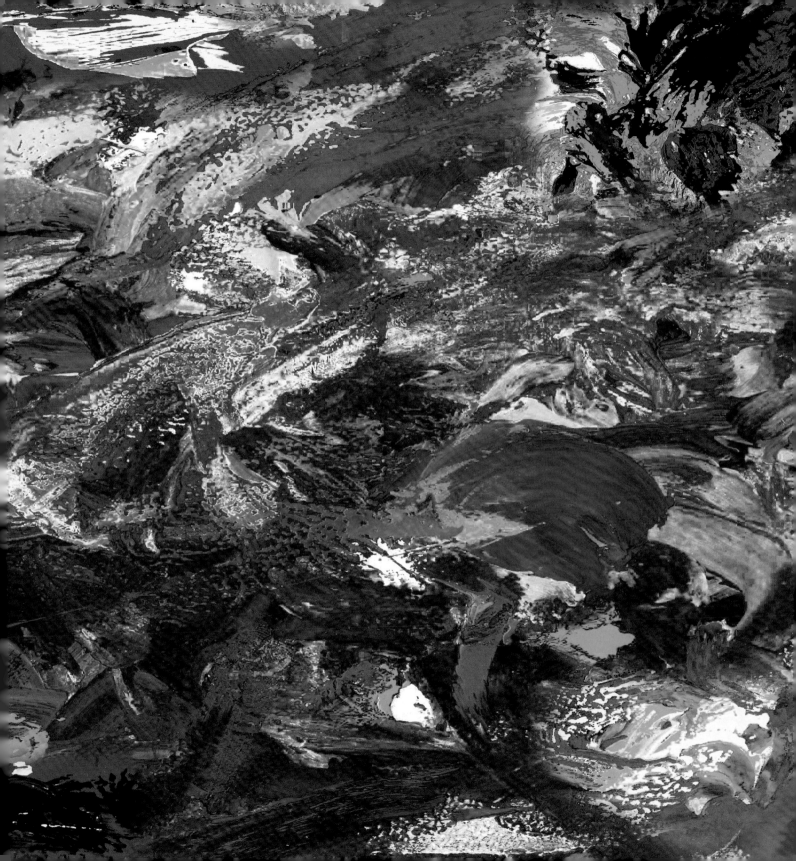

REFLECTIONS
PASSION

1. What is your purpose in life?

2. Who or what has power over you?

3. Describe the life of your dreams?

4. How do you sabotage your dreams?

5. What do you love to do? What did you love to do when you were a child?

6. What steps can you take now to find your passion in life?

People who made a Difference

Jim..this book happened because you pushed me when
I didn't believe in myself. I am forever grateful to you.

Deb.. you were there to support me through the whole process,
even when it was tough. Thank you. Thank you. Thank you. I love you.

Jeff, Michael, Al, Arvid, Mitchell, Barry & Allen...you guys keep
me sane and help me push through my pain and blocks. My life has
forever changed because of your love and support. Love you guys.

Michael & Sharon..thanks for reading, editing, suggesting and
helping me through all the versions and changes. I love you both.

Angelo...You taught me Photoshop which gave me the
tools to express my creativity in a whole new way.

Mike..thanks for printing draft copies of the book for me
so I could see how it all came together. Very cool.

Tesch...God, you are a gifted talented human being who inspires me.

Bryan..thanks for creating the Soul Miner dude. He looks cool!

Jay...thanks for helping me organize the book.

Maureen & Cinny...thanks for making the book better than
it was before you started working on it. It looks amazing!!

Books that made a Difference

Debbie Ford, *The Secret of the Shadow*
San Francisco: HarperCollins

Oriah Mountain Dreamer, *The Dance*
San Francisco: HarperCollins

Jan Goldstein, *Sacred Wounds*
New York: ReganBooks

Thomas Moore, *Dark Night of the Soul*
New York: Gotham Books

John McAfee, *The Fabric of Self*
Colorado: Woodland Publications

Hugh Prather, *The Little Book of Letting Go*
Boston: Conari Press

Don Miguel Ruiz, *The Voice of Knowledge*
San Rafael: Amber-Allen Publishing

Sharon Salzberg, *Faith*
New York: Riverhead Books

Jim Warner, *Aspirations of Greatness*
New York: John Wiley & Sons

David Richo, *Shadow Dance*
Boston: Shambhala Publications

Sabrina Ward Harrison, *Brave on the Rocks*
New York: Villard Books

Gay & Kathlyn Hendricks, *Lasting Love*
New York: Rodale

WHERE
HAVE I
BEEN